Landmark
Events in
American
History

The Scopes "Monkey" Trial

Michael V. Uschan

WORLD ALMANAC® LIBRARY

To Harry Fanning

Please visit our web site at: www.worldalmanaclibrary.com
For a free color catalog describing World Almanac® Library's list of high-quality books and multimedia programs, call 1-800-848-2928 (USA) or 1-800-387-3178 (Canada). World Almanac® Library's fax: (414) 332-3567.

Library of Congress Cataloging-in-Publication Data

Uschan, Michael V., 1948-
    The Scopes "monkey" trial / by Michael V. Uschan.
      p. cm. — (Landmark events in American history)
    Includes bibliographical references and index.
    ISBN 0-8368-5396-2 (lib. bdg.)
    ISBN 0-8368-5424-1 (softcover)
    1. Scopes, John Thomas—Trials, litigation, etc.—Juvenile literature.
  2. Evolution—Study and teaching—Law and legislation—Tennessee—
Juvenile literature. I. Title. II. Series.
    KF224.S3U825   2004
    345.73'0288—dc22   2004042796

First published in 2005 by
World Almanac® Library
330 West Olive Street, Suite 100
Milwaukee, WI 53212 USA

Copyright © 2005 by World Almanac® Library.

Produced by Discovery Books
Editor: Sabrina Crewe
Designer and page production: Sabine Beaupré
Photo researcher: Sabrina Crewe
Maps and diagrams: Stefan Chabluk
World Almanac® Library editorial direction: Mark J. Sachner
World Almanac® Library editor: Gini Holland
World Almanac® Library art direction: Tammy West
World Almanac® Library production: Jessica Morris

Photo credits: Bryan College: pp. 18 (both), 25; Corbis: cover, pp. 5, 6, 7, 8, 9, 11, 13, 14, 15, 19, 21, 22, 26, 28, 29, 30, 31, 32, 33, 34, 35, 38, 39, 40, 41, 42; The Herald News, Dayton: p. 4; Eva Cruver: pp. 16, 17, 27, 36, 43; Library of Congress: p. 24; Tennessee State Library and Archives: pp. 10, 23, 37.

Printed in Canada

1 2 3 4 5 6 7 8 9 08 07 06 05 04

Contents

Introduction

A Big Trial in a Small Town

For twelve days in July 1925, the attention of the world was focused on the tiny community of Dayton, Tennessee. The trial of high school teacher John T. Scopes for teaching **evolution** was one of the twentieth century's most sensational and important trials. During those few days, the town became the legal battleground in a social **controversy** that continues today.

The Central Issue

The question in the Scopes Trial that stirred the passions of people around the world concerned how people came to inhabit the world we live in. Did human beings evolve over millions of years from lower forms of life to their present levels of intelligence and physical ability, as scientist Charles Darwin claimed? Or were they created by God, fully formed in the space of one day, as is written in the Bible?

Although that question was what made the event so dramatic, the Scopes Trial's central issue was in fact one of freedom. Scopes was charged with breaking a Tennessee law that made the teaching of evolution illegal, and the trial was a challenge to that law. The challenge was made by people who believed the law

The *Dayton Herald* of July 23, 1925, reports the outcome of the Scopes Trial. All around the United States and in other countries, newspapers covered the sensational court case.

JURY RETURNS VERDICT OF "GUILTY" IN SCOPES CASE

The curtain dropped Tuesday noon on the world-watched, nation-wide drama entitled, "The State of Tennessee vs. John Thomas Scopes," when the jury brought in a verdict of guilty and recommended a fine of $100. It was rather anti-climax; —a relaxed finish to the bitterest legal battle ever waged in the United States—, a foretold outcome to a conflict that, earlier in the proceedings, had keyed to their highest pitch the keenest, shrewdest minds of the country.

For the state were the William Jennings Bryans—pere and sere—Attorney General Stewart, former Attorney General McKenzie, Judge J. G. McKenzie, W. C. Haggard, S. K. and H. E. Hicks. Pitted against these were Clarence Darrow, of Chicago; Dudley Field Malone, of New York; Arthur Garfield Hays, of New York; John R. Neal, of Knoxville.

Puzzling, perplexing problems confronted Judge Raulston at every turn. First came the attack on the bill of indictment. The bill stood. Then the legal squabbles over the character of testimony permissable before the jury, and a still harder clash over the introduction of expert testimony for the enlightenment of the court. In all these bitter battles the state came out victorious, but not without at least a dozen struggles that threatened on many occasions to switch from the verbal to the physical.

It was when Darrow, driven to desperation by repeated failures to have his motions sustained, attempted to put evolution on trial in the place of Scopes that the real fire-works started. The two hundred newspapermen at the trial agreed that no such oratory had ever before been heard in any courtroom. The magnetism of the brilliant Bryan, the eloquence of the oratorical Malone, the fury of the picturesque Darrow, the flowery flights of the fluent Hays, the humorous sallies of the versatile McKenzie, the forceful sentences of the earnest Stewart. It is doubtful if any case has ever assembled such an array of worthwhile speakers. But, after all the arguments were heard, the court ruled that evolution was not on trial but that the issue at the bar was, did John Scopes teach evolution in the public schools.

Came, then, the desperate effort of the defense attorneys to get before the court and the press—especially the press—the views of the

worlds greatest advocates of evolution. The bitterness of Darrow over the failure to get these expert witnesses on the stand exploded itself in an outburst towards the court that resulted in his being cited for contempt;—which citation was next day withdrawn when Darrow, after a night's reflection, made ample apologies to the court.

On account of the vast crowds here to hear the trial, Monday's session was held on a dias on the lawn; and it was at this afternoon session that Bryan, goaded by the taunts of the defense attorneys, volunteered to take the stand in defense of the Bible against science. Darrow led the attack in quizzing the great Commoner, and there always will be a division of opinion concerning the outcome of that famous battle of brains. It will be admitted by most that Bryan was at a disadvantage, in that he could only answer, and not ask questions.

One of the big surprises of the trial, that is surprise to the outside world, was the ability of Tennessee attorneys to hold their own in such brilliant company, and the able manner in which Attorney General Stewart conducted the prosecution. Friends of the Attorney General freely predict he will soon become a national figure in the legal world.

The verdict was an expected one. In fact Darrow, leading the defense, suggested to Judge Raulston that the charge to the jury be such that no division of opinion be possible among the jurymen.

An interested attendant at the trial was J. W. Butler, father of the bill against teaching evolution in the public schools of Tennessee. Mr. Butler vigorously denied that any one else but himself had aught to do with framing the bill.

"I wrote the bill while at home, on the 17 day of last December" declared Mr. Butler when told that Nashville attorneys had been credited with being the real authors of the bill. "It was on my birthday, my 49th birthday, and no one knew about my intention of introducing it except five or six of the state officials I had it typewritten by Miss Groom, stenographer in the treasurer's office and let only the five or six mentioned see it."

A peculiar phase of the famous trial that attracted the attention of the world to Dayton, is that the jury, during the eleven days of hearing, were in court little more than three hours all together.

Clarence Darrow (left) and William Jennings Bryan (right) chat in the courtroom during the Scopes Trial. Before the trial was over, Bryan and Darrow would engage in one of legal history's most dramatic and famous courtroom confrontations.

denied freedom of speech and gave government approval to one particular religion. The law, they said, violated the U.S. **Constitution** for those reasons.

Two Great Lawyers

The Scopes Trial also captivated the nation because it featured a courtroom duel between two famous men: William Jennings Bryan and Clarence Darrow. Bryan was a prominent and colorful political figure. Darrow was one of the United States' leading lawyers, well known because of the many important cases he had handled.

The Outcome of the Trial

As everyone expected, John Scopes was found guilty of breaking the law banning the teaching of evolution. The Scopes Trial had much more important consequences, however. It caused a debate about evolution that raged across the United States and other parts of the world. For years afterward, the teaching of evolution was avoided in many U.S. schools. Not until the 1960s did the U.S. **Supreme Court** challenge anti-evolution laws and address the issues of religion and freedom that had been raised by the Scopes Trial.

Open Minds
"Let the children have their minds kept open—close no door to their knowledge, shut no door from them. Make the distinction between **theology** and science. Let them have both."

Dudley Field Malone, one of the lawyers for John Scopes, July 16, 1925

Chapter 1

A Clash of Science and Faith

Changes in Daily Life

During the first few decades of the twentieth century, the way that people lived in the United States changed rapidly. Technological advances and inventions of recent decades—such as electricity, the automobile, the telephone, and the airplane—were creating new ways for people to live, work, communicate, and travel. People also enjoyed new forms of entertainment, such as movies and radio.

New Ideas and Education

It was an exciting time, and most people welcomed the modern conveniences that were making life easier. Not everyone was happy, however, that life was being transformed so swiftly. It was not

An elderly woman listens to a crystal radio set in 1924, the year before the Scopes Trial. Radio was just one of the developments that changed U.S. society in the early 1900s.

just technology but new ideas and beliefs—including the **theory** of evolution—that were changing the way people thought about themselves and the world around them.

What troubled some people in this era of great change was that many traditional beliefs and ideas were being abandoned or changed. Women had finally won the right to vote in 1920. They were becoming more independent, no longer content to let men rule their lives. In the twentieth century, for the first time in U.S. history, more people lived in cities than on farms, and they had abandoned traditional, rural ways of life. A few decades earlier, most young people only attended school for a few years. The early 1900s, however, brought new opportunities in education with the founding of public high schools in many states. By the 1920s, many more students than before were attending and graduating from high school and going on to college.

The spread of higher education brought new ideas to a wider section of the population. As younger men and women began to absorb these ideas, some of their elders became upset because what was being taught was so different from what they had learned.

Evolution Versus the Bible

Perhaps no idea was more controversial than evolution. The theory challenged something central to the lives of many people—their belief in God.

In 1859, English scientist Charles Darwin first presented his theory of evolution in his book *On the Origin of Species*. Darwin believed that all life-forms, including human beings, had gone through physical and mental developments over many years to become what

Creation

"In the beginning, God created heaven and earth. . . . And God called the dry land earth; and the gathering together of the waters called the seas. . . . And God made two great lights: the greater light to rule the day and the lesser light to rule the night: He made the stars also. . . . God created man in His own image, in the image of God, He created him; male and female He created them."

From the first chapter of Genesis, *the Bible*

The Theory of Evolution

In *On the Origin of Species* and a later book, *The Descent of Man*, Darwin explained his theory of evolution. He believed all animals and plants had evolved from simpler life-forms through millions of years and that humans, specifically, shared common ancestors with other **primates**. He claimed that the physical and mental changes that occurred in the process of evolution made it easier for living things to survive. Evolution also helped them and their descendants to compete successfully against other living things. For example, birds that developed protective coloring that helped hide them from predators had a better chance to survive and reproduce. Their descendants that had that trait would also have a greater chance of survival. Darwin called this process "natural selection."

A cartoon published in the 1870s pokes fun at evolution. In the drawing, Charles Darwin (right, holding a copy of his famous book *On the Origin of Species*) is being scolded for insulting a gorilla by claiming humans may be descended from apes.

MR. BERGH TO THE RESCUE.

THE DEFRAUDED GORILLA. "That *Man* wants to claim my Pedigree. He says he is one of my Descendants."

Mr. BERGH. "Now, Mr. DARWIN, how could you insult him so?"

they were. At first, Darwin's theory was doubted by other scientists. By the beginning of the twentieth century, however, educated people accepted the idea of evolution.

Some people, however, continued to reject Darwin's theory. It contradicted the Bible, they said, which claimed that God created the entire Universe— including human beings and all other life-forms—in just six days. Among Darwin's strongest critics were people called Christian **fundamentalists**, who maintained that every word in the Bible was true.

Other Christians were able to reconcile Darwin's theory of evolution and the concept that God created the

world. Darwin himself had written in his book that he could "see no good reason" why his ideas should "shock the religious feelings" of anyone. Christians who believed in evolution claimed God could have allowed humans to go through the evolutionary process described by Darwin. They thought, therefore, that the two differ-ing ideas of evolution and creation could both be true.

Attacking Evolution

By the early 1920s, evolution had become an accepted idea. In response, fundamentalists and others who opposed the con-cept—collectively called anti-evolutionists—became aggressive in trying to keep Darwin's theory from being taught in the United States. Among the leaders of the anti-evolution movement was William Jennings Bryan, one of the nation's most famous political figures and greatest speakers.

Self-Development

"A celebrated author has written to me that he has gradually learnt to see that it is just as noble a conception of the Deity to believe that He created a few original forms [of life] capable of self-development into other and needful forms, as to believe that He required a fresh act of creation to supply the voids caused by the action of His laws."

Charles Darwin, On the Origin of Species, *1859*

Christian Fundamentalism

Christian fundamentalists got their name from a series of pamphlets printed in 1910 entitled "The Fundamentals," which set down important things a Christian should believe. One of the fundamental beliefs was that every word of the Bible was true, which is why fundamentalists reject evolution. They believe that the authors of the Bible were inspired by God and that everything they wrote is factual rather than symbolic. One biblical story, for instance, claims a man named Jonah was swallowed by a fish, but that God several days later made the fish spit Jonah out of the fish's belly unharmed. Although some Christians think the story was written as an illustration of how God can help people, a Christian fundamentalist believes a man by that name really was swallowed by a large fish and survived.

In the 1920s, several states were considering laws to ban the teaching of evolution. In Tennessee, John Washington Butler suggested a law that became known as the Butler Act. He said schools should not teach evolution because it contradicted the Bible, which he claimed was "the foundation upon which our American government is built."

The Tennessee House of Representatives passed the act by seventy-one votes to five on January 28, 1925, but the new law still had to be approved by the state

John Washington Butler introduced the Butler Act to outlaw evolution in the Tennessee public school system.

Senate. Before the vote took place, Bryan came to Nashville, Tennessee, to support the new law. He made a fiery speech against evolution before a huge crowd. The Senate passed the Butler Act by twenty-four votes to six on March 13, 1925.

When Governor Austin Peay signed the act into law March 21, he predicted "the law will never be applied." Within a few months, he would be proved wrong.

The state capitol building in Nashville as it is today. There, in 1925, the Tennessee legislature passed the Butler Act.

11

Chapter 2

A Challenge to the Butler Act

In 1925, Dayton was a quiet community in the Cumberland Mountains, about 40 miles (64 kilometers) northeast of Chattanooga. It was an unlikely spot to gain the world's attention.

At the Drugstore

John T. Scopes, the central figure in the case, would later claim it all happened because of a "drugstore conversation that got past control." On May 4, 1925, the *Chattanooga Daily Times* printed a story about the American Civil Liberties Union (ACLU). The ACLU

Dayton is a small town in Rhea (pronounced "ray") County, Tennessee. Thousands of people descended on the town during the Scopes Trial of July 1925.

was founded in 1920 to provide help to people whose **civil rights** were being abused in one way or another. The article in the newspaper said that the organization had offered to finance a challenge to the Butler Act, which it believed was **unconstitutional**.

A Moral Town

"It would be hard to imagine a more moral town than Dayton. . . . There is no gambling. There is no place to dance. The relatively wicked, when they would indulge themselves, go to Robinson's Drug Store and debate theology."

H. L. Mencken, journalist for the Baltimore Sun *and* Mercury *newspapers, 1925*

Dayton, Tennessee

Dayton, the county seat of Rhea County in southeastern Tennessee, was typical of small southern towns in the 1920s. The community's economy was based on agriculture—strawberries were the most important local crop—and iron mining. Dayton's population had once topped 3,000, with many of that number employed by a mining company. The company went bankrupt, and by 1925 the loss of jobs had reduced the number of residents to about 1,800. Most of them lived on small farms outside the town.

At the time of the Scopes Trial, therefore, the community was not prospering. One reason businessmen in town wanted to host the trial was to boost the economy by bringing in people who would spend a lot of money at local stores and other businesses. Ultimately, the town didn't receive a long-term economic boost, but it did become famous.

Like many towns of the period, Dayton had a drugstore with a soda fountain that was a gathering place for people in the community. In Dayton, a group of businessmen met most afternoons at Robinson's Drug Store to discuss politics, religion, and the town's problems. It was at one of those meetings that the idea for the Scopes Trial was conceived.

Dayton, Tennessee, in 1925.

Some members of the original drug-store group gather for a photograph in Robinson's Drug Store in July 1925. They are (left to right): George Rappleyea, Walter White, Frank Robinson, and Clay Green.

The next day, while several friends were sipping sodas at Robinson's Drug Store, they began discussing the ACLU offer. George W. Rappleyea, who managed the Cumberland Coal and Mining Company in Dayton, was among the few Dayton residents who believed in evolution. One of the people he was talking to was Rhea County school superintendent Walter White, who rejected Darwin's theory because of his own religious views.

Hatching a Plot

The two men had argued many times before about evolution. They now began discussing whether the Butler Act was fair. Rappleyea suggested that, to settle the issue, they should take up the ACLU offer and challenge the law in court. He also argued that holding a trial on the controversial subject in Dayton would be a good way to promote the community.

The idea excited White and the others—the group included Frank Earle Robinson, the store's owner and chairman of the Rhea County school board, and lawyers Sue Hicks (who was a man) and Wallace Haggard. In what amounted to a **conspiracy**, the group decided to ask a teacher to admit to teaching evolution so that he could be charged under the Butler Act.

Choosing a Teacher

The biology teacher at Rhea County High School, W. F. Ferguson, refused to take part in the plan, and so the group asked John Scopes, a mathematics and science teacher and football coach, who had taught biology when Ferguson was ill. School had already ended for the summer—at the time the men were hatching the plan, Scopes was playing tennis with some of his students. He quickly answered their summons and met the group at Robinson's.

When Rappleyea told him about their argument over the Butler Act, Scopes claimed, "I don't see how a teacher can teach biology without teaching evolution." The group asked Scopes to help them challenge the Butler Act by saying he had taught evolution. At first, Scopes hesitated because he did not want to get in trouble with the law. But he

Influences
"How could I have [refused] considering my environmental influences? My father had read to me from Charles Darwin's *Origin of Species* and *Descent of Man*, which I had then finished reading for myself. I thought Darwin was right. It was the only plausible explanation of man's long and torturous journey to his present physical and mental development."

John T. Scopes, Center of The Storm: Memoirs of John T. Scopes, *1967*

Before the trial, John Scopes went to New York to discuss his case with members of the American Civil Liberties Union. This photo, taken during that visit, shows him reading up on legal matters in a New York law library.

15

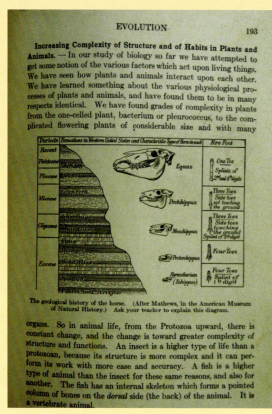

EVOLUTION 193

A page from Hunter's *A Civic Biology*.

The textbook John Scopes used when he briefly taught biology was *A Civic Biology* by George W. Hunter. The book contained an explanation of Charles Darwin's theory of evolution, although Scopes had never actually taught evolutionary theory himself. Surprisingly, the book was on a list of textbooks that state officials had approved for use in Tennessee schools six years earlier. Robinson's Drug Store sold textbooks, and so the book's explanation of evolution was readily available to anybody in Dayton who wanted to purchase it. In fact, when Scopes met with George Rappleyea in the drugstore, Rappleyea grabbed Hunter's textbook from a nearby shelf and asked Scopes if that was the one used in the classroom.

A Bad Law

"It's a bad law. Let's get rid of it. I will swear out a warrant and have you arrested. That will make a big sensation."

George W. Rappleyea to John T. Scopes, May 5, 1925

then agreed to be the **defendant** in the expected trial because he believed teachers should have the right to teach evolution.

The Charge Is Filed

Rappleyea immediately sent a telegram to the ACLU in New York City, advising them of the legal challenge to the Butler Act. The next day, the organization responded, saying it would provide financial help, legal advice, and publicity.

On May 7, when Rappleyea went to the drugstore again to show the others the telegram, they realized they had not yet filed a formal charge against Scopes. Sue Hicks and Rappleyea wrote out a **warrant** accusing Scopes of teaching evolution. Arthur Benson, a **justice of the peace** summoned by the group to Robinson's Drug Store, approved the warrant. A sheriff then served the warrant on Scopes, who was allowed to remain free.

On May 9, Scopes was formally charged in an appearance before three Rhea County justices of the peace, including Benson. He was ordered to stand trial on the charge.

In May 1925, John Scopes was charged with breaking the law when he appeared at Rhea County Courthouse in Dayton, shown here as it is today. The Scopes Trial took place in a courtroom on the second floor, on the left in this photograph.

17

The Trial Begins

A Sensational Event

When the Scopes Trial began in July 1925, it appeared as if a giant circus has taken over the normally quiet town of Dayton. In addition to the several thousand people and more than one hundred reporters who came to witness the historic clash, the streets surrounding the Rhea County Courthouse were jammed with tents set up by traveling preachers, chimpanzees trained to ride small bicycles, and vendors selling everything from hot dogs to bibles. As George Rappleyea had hoped, the trial had become a national sensation.

Monkey Business

Reporters who wrote or broadcast stories on the Scopes Trial called it the "Monkey Trial." The name came about because Darwin's theory of evolution stated that human beings shared their ancestry with other primates, an order of mammals that includes monkeys. People on both sides of the issue had fun with the thought that people were distantly related to monkeys. Newspaper cartoons used monkeys to comment humorously on the event. Frank Robinson cashed in on the idea by

Two Dayton girls hold monkey dolls sold in the town during the Scopes Trial.

serving a "Monkey Fizz" soda in his drugstore for fifteen cents. Local businesses sold stuffed monkeys and items with the caption "I'm a Monkey's Uncle." A butcher placed a sign in his window that read: "We handle all kinds of meat except monkey." There were monkeys and chimpanzees dressed in suits and ties, and people paid to have their pictures taken with the animals to prove they had been at the trial.

Joe Mendi, a celebrity chimpanzee, was brought to Dayton for the trial.

The Lawyers

The **prosecution** and **defense** both assembled teams of lawyers for the case. People were mostly interested in the two star attorneys—William Jennings Bryan and Clarence Darrow—because they were two of the most well-known men in the United States.

The defense team's star was the sixty-eight-year-old Clarence Darrow. Other lawyers defending Scopes included chief defense counsel John R. Neal, a local lawyer and law professor, Arthur G. Hays of the ACLU, and Hays's colleague Dudley Field Malone.

The sixty-five-year-old Bryan had not worked as a lawyer in more than three decades. The reporters and public still considered him the leading prosecutor, however, because he was a national spokesman against evolution, a well-known political figure, and one of the United States' great speakers. Officially in charge of the prosecution was A. Thomas Stewart, attorney general for the local judicial circuit. Other prosecutors included Bryan's son William Jennings Bryan, Jr., Sue Hicks (one of the original drugstore group), his brother Herbert B. Hicks, and Wallace Haggard (brother-in-law of druggist Frank Robinson and also one of the original group).

This photograph shows members of the legal defense team (from left to right): Clarence Darrow, Arthur Hays (standing), and Dudley Field Malone. George Rappleyea sits in the middle, with chief defense counsel John Neal on the right. A secretary (far right) is taking notes as the team prepares for court.

When Bryan came to town by train three days before the trial, more than a thousand people greeted him. Wearing a pith helmet that made him look like an African explorer, Bryan boldly proclaimed, "The trial between evolution and Christianity is a duel to the death." When Darrow arrived two days later he told reporters, "John Scopes isn't on trial, civilization is on trial."

The Trial Begins

The Scopes Trial began on Friday, July 10. More than one thousand people jammed into the small, second-floor courtroom, with three hundred of them having to stand. The first day was devoted to **jury** selection, which only took two-and-a-half hours. Rhea County Judge John T. Raulston then called a recess until Monday, July 13.

Broadcasting history was made when the trial's second day began. On July 13, Chicago radio station WGN broadcast the event nationally, something that had never been done before. Due to problems setting up radio microphones, the morning session began a few minutes late. That did not bother Judge Raulston, who proudly boasted, "My gavel will be heard around the world."

Four-year-old Tommy Brewer sits on the clerk's desk in the courtroom to pull names out of a hat. This was the method used to choose prospective jurors. Brewer died in 2003, the last living participant in the Scopes Trial.

The people selected to serve on the jury for the Scopes Trial assemble for a photograph before the trial begins. On the right is John Raulston, the trial's judge.

The Defense Opens

The defense opened on July 13 by arguing that the case should be dismissed because the Butler Act violated the U.S. and Tennessee Constitutions. Several attorneys argued various points of law concerning Scopes' right to teach something most people believed was

The Butler Act and the Constitution

Clarence Darrow never expected successfully to defend John Scopes, whom he knew would be convicted of violating the Butler Act. Darrow, in fact, wanted a conviction so that he could make an **appeal** to the U.S. Supreme Court. In that appeal, he intended to prove the Butler Act was unconstitutional. Under the Fourteenth **Amendment**, states are not allowed to make laws that deny citizens their freedoms and rights. Two of these rights, laid out in the First Amendment to the Constitution, are free speech and the right to worship in any faith. Darrow's basic argument would be that the Tennessee law denied Scopes freedom of speech by making it illegal for him to teach an accepted scientific theory. He would also argue that the law was unconstitutional because Tennessee had no right to teach Christianity, or indeed any other faith, as the one and only religion.

21

Clarence Darrow raises his arm while speaking at the Scopes Trial. On July 13, he told the court that Tennessee had no moral or legal right to ban the teaching of evolution.

true. Their arguments were overshadowed that afternoon by Darrow, who delivered a brilliant, impassioned speech in which he claimed the law was "as brazen and bold an attempt to destroy learning as was ever made in the Middle Ages."

Darrow also charged that Bryan was as much to blame for "this foolish, mischievous, and wicked act" as anyone because he had helped win passage of the Butler Act. His remark brought gasps from Bryan's supporters in the courtroom as well as from thousands of people outside listening to the trial on loudspeakers.

Dismissal Denied

The prosecution lawyers did not even try to answer Darrow's arguments. On July 15, however, Judge Raulston ruled that the Butler Act did not violate the Constitution—the case would not be dismissed as Darrow had requested. Raulston's ruling was expected because he was known to oppose evolution. After the trial, Raulston admitted, "If I lose faith in *Genesis*, I'm afraid I'll lose faith in the rest of the Bible."

Prosecution Witnesses

After the opening statements, the prosecution began calling **witnesses** to **testify**. The first was Rhea County school superintendent Walter White. He declared that Scopes admitted to him in Robinson's Drug Store that he had taught evolution.

The key witnesses were students from the classes Scopes had taught—fourteen-year-old Howard Morgan and seventeen-year-old Harry Shelton. Both testified that Scopes explained the theory of evolution.

The last witness was Frank Robinson, who said that, in his drugstore, he sold the same textbook Scopes had used and that it explained Darwin's theory. A. Thomas Stewart, who led the prosecution, finished the prosecution's case by reading from *Genesis*, the Biblical account of creation.

Defense Witnesses

In the afternoon session of July 15, the defense began its case. Darrow planned to call a series of experts to talk about science and religion. They would explain that Charles Darwin's theory of

Evolving Organism

"A little germ of one-celled organism formed [in the sea], and this organism kept evolving until it got to be a pretty good-sized animal and them came on to be a land animal, and it kept on evolving, and from this was man."

Howard Morgan, July 15, 1925, testifying about what John Scopes taught in biology class

While witnesses testified inside the courthouse, a fundamentalist preacher addresses a crowd outside about the dangers of teaching evolution.

23

While the nation's attention was focused on Dayton, newspapers made fun of the town. This cartoon showed "evolution in Tennessee" as a sleepy town turning into a media circus.

EVOLUTION IN TENNESSEE

evolution was believed by educated people, including Christians, and that it did not necessarily conflict with the Bible.

The first witness was Dr. Maynard Metcalf, a nationally known zoologist as well as a leader in the Congregational Church. Metcalf testified that of all the scientists in the United States, "I know there is not a single one among them that doubts the fact of evolution."

Expert Testimony

Metcalf had not finished testifying on July 15 when the afternoon session ended. The next day, however, when Darrow tried to continue questioning him, Stewart objected on behalf of the prosecution, saying that testimony about evolution had no bearing on the case and should not be permitted.

The trial came to a halt because of this dispute over courtroom procedure. The jurors were taken out of the courtroom, and attorneys for both sides began to argue whether expert testimony on evolution should be allowed.

For the rest of the morning session on July 16, members of the prosecution argued against the use of such testimony. Stewart claimed that the only valid question in the trial was whether Scopes had broken the law, not whether evolution was true.

Courtroom Prayer

On the first day of the trial, Clarence Darrow was angry because a minister was allowed to say a prayer before the session began. Darrow said he had never seen that happen in any other court. He was upset because he believed prayer might influence the case, which centered on religion. Darrow, however, did not officially object to the prayer until July 14, the third day of the trial, when he told Judge Raulston he did not think it was right to have someone pray in court. The judge ruled against Darrow and continued to allow prayers to open each session.

A headline in the *New York Journal* about the prayer issue at the Scopes Trial.

Dudley Field Malone presents the case for scientific evidence on July 16. In arguments that were both passionate and logical, Malone said the witnesses should "have a right to testify in support of our view that the Bible is not to be taken literally as an authority in a court of law."

Brilliant Speeches

After a lunch recess, Bryan gave his first speech of the trial. He eloquently attacked evolution while arguing that testimony on the theory had no bearing on the case. It was the moment his admirers in court and outside had been waiting for since the trial began. They accompanied his dramatic arguments with loud "Amens!"—as if they were in church listening to a sermon—and they applauded enthusiastically when he finished.

After Bryan's dramatic performance, Dudley Field Malone gave a brilliant speech for the defense, claiming testimony of the expert witnesses should be allowed. His speech was so powerful that Malone, like Bryan, was greeted with thunderous applause when he finished. But there was only one listener who counted: Judge Raulston. And no one would know until the next day how he felt about the issue.

Raulston Rules

The next day, July 17, Raulston ruled that he would not allow expert witnesses to testify because science and religion were "not the issue" in the trial. Raulston said the only matter that had to be decided was whether Scopes had taught evolution in violation of the Butler Act.

The defense then asked if it could read out some **affidavits** from the witnesses. Because the ruling had only covered witnesses testifying before jurors, Judge Raulston allowed the request. But when

Darrow asked for the remainder of the day to collect the affidavits, Raulston objected. He said the testimony had to be read into the court record immediately.

Angered by the refusal, an emotional Darrow told Raulston he could not understand why the judge was rejecting nearly every defense request. Believing that Darrow had criticized him for favoring the prosecution, Raulston said, "I hope you do not mean to reflect [negatively] upon the court." To which Darrow, his anger overruling his good judgment, sarcastically responded, "Well, your honor has the right to hope."

The judge became so angry that he halted the trial until Monday. But he did not end the day before reminding Darrow that "I have the right to do something else." The statement was a warning that he could charge Darrow with **contempt of court**.

Was the Trial Over?

Because the experts were the only witnesses the defense had, the trial appeared to be over. In fact, many journalists left town that weekend because they did not think anything exciting would happen except for the **verdict**, which they knew would be "guilty."

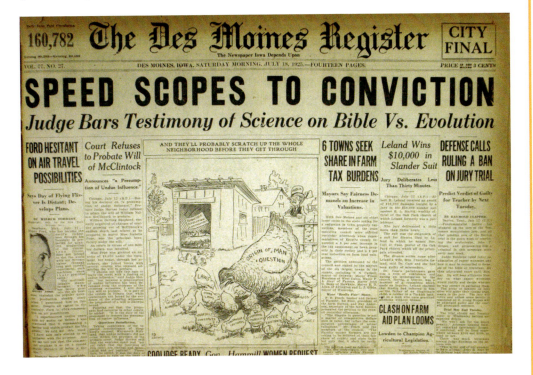

The *Des Moines Register* announces Judge Raulston's ruling against scientific evidence. Because of this ruling, everyone, including newspaper reporters, thought the case would be over.

Darrow and Bryan

On Monday July 20, the courtroom was again packed with one thousand spectators. They were so excited that court official Kelso Rice had trouble getting them to be quiet. "Sit down. This ain't no circus," Rice warned them.

Contempt Charge

The trial's most exciting day opened with a startling announcement by Judge Raulston: He was charging Darrow with contempt of court for apparently having questioned the judge's fairness on July 17. The declaration created a sensational start to the day's proceedings. (That afternoon, the judge dropped the charge after Darrow humbly apologized and shook his hand, a display that drew applause from spectators.)

Sweltering Conditions

William Jennings Bryan, stripped down in the courtroom.

The Scopes Trial was conducted during a hot spell in which courtroom temperatures often topped 100°F (38°C). Because the courtroom did not have ceiling fans to cool participants, Judge Raulston allowed attorneys to take off their jackets and ties and roll up their shirtsleeves. People tried to cool themselves by waving palm leaf fans, but the heat was intense, causing one defense attorney to faint during the trial. The court did have one small electric fan, placed next to the judge.

The Courtroom Moves

After a break for lunch, Raulston had a second dramatic announcement. The weight of the huge crowds had caused cracks in the first-floor ceiling below the courtroom, so he was moving the trial outside for fear the floor could collapse and also because of the tremendous heat. Said Raulston: "I think the court should adjourn downstairs."

Everyone moved onto the courthouse lawn. The judge, attorneys, defendant, and court officials were seated on a raised platform usually used by ministers to deliver sermons. Spectators and journalists gathered around the platform. They sat on wooden benches, in nearby cars, or on the grass.

A Surprise Witness

Darrow then stunned the crowd of some five thousand people by asking Bryan to testify. He said he wanted a Bible expert to explain why the theory of evolution was false, since that was the reason the Butler Act would not allow it to be taught. The prosecution opposed the request. But when Bryan agreed to testify, Raulston allowed it. The result was a dramatic confrontation that the *New York Times* newspaper claimed was "the most amazing court scene in Anglo-Saxon history."

Judge Raulston was a devout Baptist Christian. Darrow accused him of favoring the prosecution, but the judge tried to keep the trial proceedings fair.

An Apology
"I am quite certain that the remark should not have been made, and the Court could not help taking notice of it. I am sorry that I made it. I want to apologize to the court for it."

Clarence Darrow, apology in court, July 20, 1925

Clarence Darrow (1857–1938)

Clarence Darrow during the Scopes Trial.

Clarence Darrow was born in Ohio and became a lawyer at twenty-one years old. After several years as an attorney for the Chicago and Northwestern Railroad, Darrow switched sides when, in 1895, he resigned from the railroad to defend railway union leader Eugene Debs and other union officials after the 1894 Pullman Strike, a significant event in labor history. Darrow went on to become famous for the many labor cases he handled. Because he opposed the death penalty, he also defended more than fifty people accused of murder. His most famous trial, apart from the Scopes case, was his defense in 1924 of Nathan Leopold and Richard Loeb, who had confessed to killing a young boy "for the thrill of it." Darrow was able to win them life sentences instead of the death penalty. Darrow was a declared agnostic, a person who neither believes nor disbelieves in the existence of a god. Throughout his life, he remained a defender of the rights of labor unions and of free thought and expression.

Biblical Truths

Darrow began by asking Bryan if he knew a lot about the Bible. "Yes, I have studied the Bible for about fifty years," responded Bryan. Bryan's testimony began with the claim that "everything in the Bible should be accepted as given there." Darrow asked if that meant he believed a fish actually swallowed Jonah and that Jonah emerged from it unharmed three days later. Bryan said he did.

Darrow asked Bryan if he knew the date of the flood recounted in the Bible, in which all life on Earth was wiped out except for

Noah, his family, and animals he placed on his ark. Bryan said a biblical expert had calculated it happened in 4004 B.C., or six thousand years ago. Bryan even gave the date and time when the flood began: October 23 at 9:00 A.M. When Darrow stated that people in countries such as Egypt and China had histories extending further back in time than that, Bryan said he did not believe such claims.

Confusion and Embarrassment

During an hour of tough questioning, Darrow tried to make Bryan look foolish and confused. When Darrow asked Bryan if he knew how the date of the flood had been calculated, Bryan said he did not. "I do not think about things I don't think about," Bryan said. When Darrow asked, "Do you think about things you *do* think about?" Bryan answered, "Well, sometimes."

When the trial moved outside on July 20, a huge crowd assembled on the courthouse lawn. The spectators witnessed Darrow's fierce questioning of Bryan.

William Jennings Bryan (1860—1925)

William Jennings Bryan was born in Salem, Illinois. After becoming a lawyer in 1883, he moved to Lincoln, Nebraska. It was there that Bryan, a Democrat, began a political career that included two terms in the House of Representatives (from 1890) and unsuccessful campaigns for the presidency in 1896, 1900, and 1908. Bryan, famed for his kindness and compassion as well as his public speaking, was a great supporter of poor working people, especially farmers, and he campaigned for a minimum wage, the vote for women, and other reforms that would help workers. He became U.S. Secretary of State in 1912 but resigned the post in 1915 because he was a **pacifist** and believed President Woodrow Wilson was leading the nation into war. In later life, Bryan devoted himself to moral and religious causes, campaigning against the sale of alcohol and against the teaching of evolution.

The buttons above and right were used by Bryan at different times in political campaigns.

Even though most spectators were Bryan's supporters, many began laughing. It appeared Bryan was admitting that he did not think carefully about many things he believed. The answer disappointed his admirers and embarrassed Bryan, who was not accustomed to being laughed at.

A photograph, taken from above, shows the trial taking place outside on July 20. Bryan is seated on the left during Darrow's questioning and is holding a fan with which to cool himself. Darrow is standing center right.

The Length of a Day

The next line of questioning concerned the length of a biblical day. Darrow asked Bryan, "Do you think the Earth was made in six days?" Bryan amazed his inquisitor and everyone else by answering, "Not six days of twenty-four hours." An astonished Darrow asked, "Doesn't it say so [in the Bible]?" to which Bryan said, "No sir."

Days or Periods

Darrow: "Do you think [days in the Bible] were literal days?"

Bryan: "My impression is they were periods."

Darrow: "Have you any idea of the length of the periods?"

Bryan: "No. I don't."

Darrow: "If you call those periods, they may have been a very long time?"

Bryan: "They might have been."

Darrow: "The Creation might have been going on for a very long time."

Bryan: "It might have continued for millions of years."

Testimony of William Jennings Bryan, July 20, 1925

Bryan had many supporters in Dayton during the trial. Evangelist T. T. Martin sold Bryan's works and Martin's own book, *Hell and the High School*, which warned against "the deadly, soul-destroying poison of Evolution."

Bryan then said a biblical day might have lasted "millions of years." The answer shocked many in the crowd who believed that every word in the Bible was absolutely true, and thus a "day" in biblical terms had to be a day as they knew it. Bryan had betrayed the fundamentalist principle of believing every single word in the Bible. Even worse, the answer suggested that the biblical account of creation could have lasted long enough to allow for Charles Darwin's theory of evolution.

The Trial Is Adjourned

After more questions, Bryan finally snapped in anger. He stood up, shook his fist in the air, and accused Darrow of trying to "slur the Bible." When Darrow roared back that he was only trying to show Bryan believed in "fool ideas that no intelligent Christian on Earth believes," almost everyone on the courthouse lawn began shouting and arguing with each other. Fearing a riot, Raulston excused Bryan as a witness. He then **adjourned** the trial until 9:00 A.M. the next day.

The Verdict

On July 21, the trial moved back inside the courthouse. When Raulston opened the trial that day, he said he would remove Bryan's testimony of the previous day from the court record. The judge said it would shed no light on the issues involved if they were later presented in an appeal. Then Stewart and Darrow summed up their cases for the jurors. Darrow did something no defense lawyer is supposed to do—he asked that John Scopes be found guilty. He wanted a guilty verdict so he could appeal it in the Supreme Court and have the law ruled unconstitutional.

The jurors began considering the case at 11:14 A.M. Eight or nine minutes later, they returned with a guilty verdict, as Darrow had hoped. Scopes made a brief statement, the first words he had spoken during the course of the trial. Judge Raulston then fined him $100, and the Scopes Trial was over.

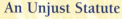

An Unjust Statute
"Your honor, I feel that I have been convicted of violating an unjust statute. I will continue in the future as I have in the past, to oppose this law in any way I can. Any other action would be in violation of my ideal of academic freedom—that is, to teach the truth as guaranteed in our Constitution."

John T. Scopes, July 21, 1925

The jury only took a few minutes to return a verdict. This photo shows Scopes (left) with Dudley Field Malone, listening to the jury's verdict.

After the Trial

During the trial, Frank Robinson promoted his drugstore and the part it played in Dayton's greatest event. After the trial ended, Dayton soon went back to its normal, quiet routine.

Over a period of two weeks, nearly 150 reporters had written 2 million words, traveling ministers had preached against evolution, and spectators had filled the streets of Dayton to overflowing. Suddenly, they all left town. Peace and quiet descended once again on the small community.

A Sudden Death

The guilty verdict was a victory for William Jennings Bryan, but he knew he had been humiliated. Newspaper stories about the trial ridiculed Bryan for allowing Darrow to trap him into answers that made him abandon his literal interpretation of the Bible.

Bryan remained in Dayton, where he wrote articles and traveled locally to make speeches about the case. On July 26, Bryan ate lunch in Dayton and then took a nap from which he never awoke—while sleeping, he suffered a stroke and died. When reporters asked Darrow about the death, they suggested Bryan had died of a broken heart. "Broken heart nothing—he died of a busted belly," Darrow said cruelly of Bryan, a large man who loved to eat. Then he continued more kindly, "His death is a great loss to the American people."

The Appeal

The goal of the defense had always been to have the Tennessee and U.S. Supreme Courts decide if the Butler Act was constitutional. In January 1926, the defense team from the Scopes Trial made an appeal to the Tennessee Supreme Court. Darrow and other attorneys for both sides appeared in the state capital of Nashville in May of that year to argue about the Butler Act before the high court.

When the justices issued their ruling January 15, 1927, however, the defense received a nasty surprise. At the end of the original trial, Judge Raulston had set the fine, even though Tennessee law required a jury to impose any fines greater than $50. The fine had been set at $100, however, and the Tennessee Supreme Court used

What Happened to John Scopes?

John Scopes was mainly a spectator at his own trial, but it still made him famous. Afterward, Scopes was offered thousands of dollars to lecture on evolution before paying audiences. But as Scopes wrote in his memoirs, "I knew I would not live happily in a spotlight." Instead of cashing in on his fame, Scopes quit teaching and studied geology at the University of Chicago. He then worked for more than thirty years as an oil and gas engineer in Venezuela and later in Louisiana. Scopes died in 1970.

John Scopes (left), with his father, sits on the porch of the house where he was living during the trial.

this fact as an excuse to reverse the verdict. Because there was no longer a guilty verdict, the case could not be appealed. The defense, therefore, never had the chance to prove the Butler Act was unconstitutional in the U.S. Supreme Court.

Shunning Evolution

In the two years after the trial, Mississippi and Arkansas passed anti-evolution laws similar to Tennessee's. Although the heated emotions of the Scopes Trial began to fade in a few years, the controversy never died. The outcome of the trial led many textbook publishers to delete material on evolution because they feared school districts would not buy their science books. New editions of *A Civic Biology*, the textbook used in Dayton, did not mention evolution.

For many years, teachers in some areas of the country, mainly the South, would not teach Darwin's theory even if their states allowed it. They feared trouble with parents or school boards if they told students about evolution.

A group of students sit at desks in the 1940s. From the 1920s to the 1950s, many U.S. public schools avoided the teaching of evolution.

The United States launched its first satellite, *Explorer I*, in 1958, the year after the first Soviet satellite went into space. The next year, the U.S. government began to push for improved science education to compete with the Soviets.

Evolution Comes Back

After 1957, the U.S. government became committed to improving science education. The renewed emphasis on science came after the Soviet Union beat the United States into space that year by launching *Sputnik*, the first satellite to orbit the Earth. U.S. officials wanted better education so the nation could improve its space program.

In 1959, on the hundredth anniversary of the publication of *On the Origin of Species*, a group of scientists and teachers sponsored by the federal government proclaimed that "one hundred years without evolution is enough." The group, which had made a study of science education in the United States, recommended that all textbooks include the theory and all schools teach it.

Tennessee's Reputation

In 1959, however, it was still illegal to teach evolution in Tennessee. Attempts to repeal the Butler Act had failed in 1935 and 1952, and the Tennessee state legislature did not overturn the law until May 16, 1967. A newspaper editorial said the move was long overdue:

"Tennessee will be saved the ordeal of another trial in which a proud state is required to make a monkey of itself in a court of law."

Many people believe the state of Tennessee was the biggest loser in the Scopes Trial. Opposing the teaching of evolution made the state appear backward for refusing to accept modern science. Tennessee unfairly won a reputation for being uncultured and anti-education.

Supreme Court Rulings

A year after Tennessee acted, the U.S. Supreme Court finally issued a decision that struck down laws opposing the teaching of evolution. In 1964, Susan Epperson, a biology teacher at Little Rock Central High School, claimed the Arkansas anti-evolution law passed in 1927 was unconstitutional. On November 12, 1968, in *Epperson v. Arkansas*, Supreme Court justices ruled that the Arkansas law contradicted what is known as the Establishment clause in the First Amendment.

Many years later, in 1987, another important ruling was made by the Supreme Court in the case *Edwards v. Aguillard*. A law in Louisiana required teachers who taught evolution to teach their students about the biblical version of creation, too. The two ideas had to be taught together, as opposing scientific theories. The court said that evolution could be taught in public schools because it was a science, whereas **creationism** could not be taught because it was a religious belief.

The Constitution and Bill of Rights (the first ten amendments) are housed in the National Archives in Washington, D.C. The First Amendment states that everyone should have freedom of speech and religion.

Because of rulings in the Supreme Court, students in public schools today are entitled to learn about evolution and other scientific theories. Public schools are not allowed to teach any one religion to their students, who come from many different faiths.

Schools and Religion

The Establishment clause in the First Amendment says: "Congress shall make no law respecting an establishment of religion, or prohibiting the free exercise thereof; . . ." The clause can be used to argue both sides of the debate about religion in schools. It says clearly that the government must not involve itself with religion, an argument used by evolutionists. It also says, however, that the government must not interfere with people's right to practice their religions. That point has been used by religious groups protesting the banning of any and all religion from public schools.

In the two Supreme Court cases that challenged laws concerning the teaching of evolution, one point was clear. Public schools are part of government, and as such they should not get involved in religion. This is what people mean when they talk about separation of church and state. Although some fundamental Christians wanted schools to teach creationism to balance the teaching of evolution, it was based on a religious belief and therefore should not be allowed, said the Supreme Court. Not only did the teaching of creationism flout the Establishment clause, but it prohibited the free exercise of religion because it gave only the Christian Bible's version of creation, not those of other faiths. On the other side, creationists argued (and still do) that evolution is only a theory and should not be presented to students as proven fact.

Conclusion

Dayton Today

Robinson's Drug Store in Dayton is long gone. But visitors to the town today can tour the Rhea County Courthouse, now a national historic landmark. In the second-floor courtroom where the Scopes Trial was held, they can sit in chairs used by the trial's participants and view displays about the trial.

Residents of Dayton are proud of their past. A re-creation of the trial has been performed at the courthouse several times. Together with Bryan College—a Christian college that opened in Dayton in 1930 as a memorial to William Jennings Bryan—the town holds a four-day Scopes Trial Festival every year.

The Debate Continues

The Scopes Trial reflected a great clash in American society between religious tradition and scientific progress. The debate continues today. In 1999, Kansas officials removed evolution

The movie *Inherit the Wind*, based on a 1955 play of the same name, premiered in Dayton in 1960. Spencer Tracy (left) played Darrow and Fredric March (right) took the part of Bryan.

In the Rhea County Courthouse, the courtroom where the Scopes Trial took place, pictured here in 2003, has been preserved as it was in the 1920s.

as a subject for statewide testing. This does not ban teaching evolution, but it makes it less likely teachers will take time to explain it.

Another scientific idea about the creation of life, the big-bang theory, has developed since the Scopes Trial. The big-bang theory puts forward the idea that the Universe was created in an explosion of matter billions of years ago. Scientists freely admit the theory is still under development, but discussion of it troubles Christian fundamentalists and is avoided in many schools.

The Legacy of the Scopes Trial

The legacy of the Scopes Trial is a mixed one. At first, the guilty verdict strengthened opponents of Charles Darwin's theory in their fight to keep evolution from being taught. The result was that many schools avoided the subject for more than three decades. However, news reports on the trial publicized the idea of evolution, bringing it to the attention of millions of people who had never heard of it. And the effort to overturn the Butler Act, even though it failed at the Scopes Trial, eventually led to new legal challenges that would succeed in showing that such laws were unconstitutional.

Time Line

1859 ■ *On the Origin of Species* by Charles Darwin is published.

1925 ■ March 21: Butler Act is signed into law in Tennessee.
May 5: John T. Scopes agrees to help challenge the Butler Act.
May 7: Warrant is issued against John T. Scopes.
July 10: Scopes Trial begins in Dayton, Tennessee.
July 13: Clarence Darrow argues that the Butler Act is unconstitutional and asks for the case to be dismissed.
July 15: Judge Raulston declares the Butler Act constitutional, and the trial continues.
July 16: William Jennings Bryan argues against allowing the defense to have scientific and religious experts testify on evolution.
July 17: Judge Raulston forbids defense's expert witnesses to testify.
July 20: Darrow calls Bryan to testify as a Bible expert.
July 21: The jury finds Scopes guilty and Judge Raulston fines him $100.
July 26: Bryan dies in Dayton.

1926 ■ January: Scopes Trial defense team makes an appeal to Tennessee Supreme Court.
May 31: Tennessee Supreme Court hears arguments on the constitutionality of the Butler Act.

1927 ■ January 17: Tennessee Supreme Court reverses Scopes' conviction.

1930 ■ September: Bryan College, named for William Jennings Bryan, opens in Dayton.

1955 ■ *Inherit the Wind*, a play about the Scopes Trial, opens in New York City.

1959 ■ U.S. government study group recommends the teaching of evolution in all schools.

1960 ■ July 21: Dayton celebrates the thirty-fifth anniversary of the Scopes Trial with the movie premiere of *Inherit the Wind*.

1967 ■ May 16: Tennessee overturns the Butler Act.

1968 ■ In the case *Epperson v. Arkansas*, the U.S. Supreme Court overturns an Arkansas ban on teaching evolution.

1987 ■ In the case *Edwards v. Aguillard*, the U.S. Supreme Court overturns a Louisiana law that states biblical creationism must be taught alongside evolution.

Glossary

adjourn: stop proceedings until a later time or day.

affidavit: statement made and sworn as true in front of an official.

amendment: change or addition; in the case of the U.S. Constitution, amendments are additions to the original document.

appeal: ask a higher court to examine a trial verdict and overturn it.

civil rights: basic rights—such as freedom, education, and choice of religion and political beliefs—of every person.

conspiracy: secret plot or agreement among a group of people.

constitution: basic rules of government for a nation.

contempt of court: showing of disrespect to a court or judge.

controversy: issue that causes a lot of discussion and disagreement.

creationism: belief in bibilical creation as a scientific fact.

defendant: person charged with a crime.

defense: legal representative who speaks in favor of a defendant.

evolution: process of change in living things over a long period of time.

fundamentalist: person who believes strongly in following the basic rules of a religion and in a strict interpretation of religious writings.

jury: panel of twelve people who decide whether a defendant is guilty or innocent.

justice of the peace: local official with certain legal powers, such as committing people to trial and performing marriages.

pacifist: person who is opposed to violence and war under all circumstances.

primate: order of mammals that includes humans, apes, and monkeys.

prosecution: legal representative who presents the case against a defendant in a trial in order to prove him or her guilty.

Supreme Court: highest court in the United States or in each state. The U.S. Supreme Court has the power to make final decisions on matters of law and interpretation of the U.S. Constitution.

testify: give evidence at a trial.

theology: study of religion.

theory: reasonable or scientifically sound idea that is used to explain something. Theories can become accepted as fact when they have been shown to work over a period of time and there is enough evidence to support them.

unconstitutional: action or law that disagrees with the principles of the U.S. Constitution.

verdict: decision made by the jury in a trial.

warrant: document authorizing an arrest or other official action.

witness: person who experiences something or sees an incident take place and confirms in a court that it happened.

Further Information

Books

Caudill, Edward. *The Scopes Trial: A Photographic History*. University of Tennessee Press, 2000.

Hamilton, Virginia. *In the Beginning: Creation Stories from Around the World*. Harcourt, 1988.

Hanson, Freya Ottem. *The Scopes Monkey Trial* (Headline Court Cases). Enslow, 2000.

Jenkins, Steve. *Life on Earth: The Story of Evolution*. Houghton Mifflin, 2002.

Scopes, John T. and James Presley. *Center of the Storm: Memoirs of John T. Scopes*. Holt, Rinehart and Winston, 1967.

Web Sites

www.bryan.edu/historical/index.html Bryan College web site has articles about and photographs of the Scopes Trial.

www.law.umkc.edu/faculty/projects/ftrials/scopes/scopes.htm University of Missouri Famous Trials web site is a wonderful resource for information on the Scopes Trial and over thirty other famous trials.

www.pbs.org/wgbh/amex/monkeytrial/ Public television web site with information, photographs, and audio and video links to do with the Scopes Trial.

Useful Addresses

American Civil Liberties Union
125 Broad Street, 18th Floor
New York, NY 10004
Telephone: (212) 549-2500

Rhea County Courthouse and Museum
1475 Market Street
Dayton, TN 37321
Telephone: (423) 775-7801

Index

Page numbers in *italics* indicate maps and diagrams. Page numbers in **bold** indicate other illustrations.